This Is the Day
We've Been Waiting For

Poems

by

Dudley Laufman

This Is the Day We've Been Waiting For
Copyright © 2017 by Dudley Laufman

Photographs, book cover design & editorial assistance by Lindsay Holden of Canterbury, New Hampshire

Cover photo taken at sunrise at Pemaquid Point Lighthouse Pemaquid Maine, June 2016

Author photograph, back cover, Rail Trail Chichester, New Hampshire, Fall 2016

www.lindsayholdenphotography.com

Published by Piscataqua Press
An imprint of RiverRun Bookstore, Inc.
142 Fleet Street | Portsmouth, NH | 03801
www.riverrunbookstore.com
www.piscataquapress.com

ISBN: 978-1-944393-47-2
Printed in the United States of America

Other poetry books and chapbooks by Dudley Laufman

Currently Available:
>The Stone Man (Canterbury Shaker Village, 2005)
>Walking Sticks (Beech River Books, 2007)
>Behind the Beat (Puddinghouse, 2008)
>She Plumb Ned, She More'n Plumb
>>(Beech River Books, 2011)
>Islandia Fables & Poems (Longhouse, 2015)
>Bull & More Bull (Longhouse, 2016)

Out of Print:
>I Hear Ringing Reels (Wind in the Timothy Press, 1962)
>The Wolfhunters (Self, 1964)
>Beg of Foxes (Gibson's Book Store, 1966)
>Wind in the Timothy (Self, 1965)
>Wee Herd's Whistle (Vermont Stoveside Press, 1967)
>Of The Fern (Self, 1973)
>An Orchard & A Garden (William Bauhan Press, 1974)
>A Dancing Master's Diary (Self, 1981)
>The Magic Pochette (Self, 1981)
>Mouth Music (Wind in the Timothy Press, 2001)
>How Contra-Dancing Was Invented
>>(Wind in theTimothy Press, 2002)
>I Was a Fiddler Before I Came Here (Self, 2002)
>Bull (Wind in the Timothy Press, 2003)
>Smoke Screen (A Pudding House Chapbook, 2004)
>In the Southwest Corner (Puddinghouse, 2008)

For a complete list of the author's work, please visit:
www.dudleylaufman.com
www.windinthetimothypress.com

or you may write to the author at:
PO Box 61
Canterbury, NH 03224
dudleylaufman@gmail.com

ACKNOWLEDGEMENTS

Some of these poems have appeared previously
in the following magazines, journals and exhibits:

Exit 13
Echoes
Facebook
Chrysalis
Fiddler Magazine
Country Dance & Song
Patterns
Touchstone
Avocet
Silt Reader
Open Spaces
South Boston Literary Gazette
The Canterbury Newsletter
Village Rising

for Indian Summer

for Abandoned roads

for IPH

TABLE OF CONTENTS

ABANDONED ROAD

I never think of myself as abandoned. Gates and Bars maybe but not abandoned. Even though there is an end to me (I come out someplace, someone's back yard), I am long and have history in my mulch.

I have stone walls on both sides. I dip down deep into the dark forest. Road to long ago, trod on by natives, deer-skinned musket carriers. Penacooks jogged to hunt, colonists to pioneer. I just go to go.

I am on the map. A dotted line weaving through the elevation curves that makes me famous. About halfway I am pinned on a pasture high as a crow's caw.

At one point I merge with an exempt railroad track. The engineers used my foundation where I followed the straight and narrow through a gorge with blue ice. I don't think of trains. I am a tunneling green wreath.

The trains veered off onto a switchback so it could gain the hill. I go straight up the steep incline into the edge of town.

On the return I see what the eyes in the back of my head missed before. Cardinal flowered herons by a brook. Old logging road (no stone walls like I have). Cellar hole with lilacs near the high pasture (they must have wanted the view). When the farm failed I was closed. There was a better way to get to town. No jeeps or wagons now. Snowmobiles, ATVs, horses, hunters, foot traffic....here comes one now, knapsack and walking stick.

Sometimes I wish I went to a tidal inlet but that is another road.

1

BRIDGE

On the way to town I take a back road, mostly gravel,
in preference to the highway. Passes through several
swamps, leaves first to turn in the fall, below a rock studded
pasture with black and white bullocks grazing, and by a
logging operation, skidder parked beside the road. A few
homes tucked in the woods. I am not sure how these folks
like the dust, the ruts, pot holes, mud, the grader straightening
it all out every season. Maybe they would vote to have it
tarred.

I love it the way it is, would vote against paving. There is a
narrow bridge good for only one car at a time. Occasionally
I will meet one there. We sit at either end beckoning the
other on. He or she is probably a local, tired of the dirt road?
There is no meeting halfway on this issue.

ELBOW

What was once a pasture is now my two acre small
holding settled in the elbow crook of an L shaped
stone wall. The rocks must have come from the large
hayfield on the other side, nobody in their right mind
would move stones from a pasture.

I sometimes borrow some of the smaller rocks to hold
down the windswept black plastic mulch that does my weeding
these days although I occasionally lay it back so I can use
the three pronged cultivator, see the soil roll away like waves
from a boat.

I sit in the garden, my medium size, lightly callused hands,
wrapped around a G&T (or a V&T if it is in the fall) but hands
not as large or rough as the Shaker hands that wrassled these now
lichened rocks from stoneboat to wall.

SOLSTICE

There is this solstice thing we do
around the wintery fire,
in a clearing in the woods
to make the sun climb higher.

The bonfire warmth grows wider,
further out, further out,
into spring and summertime
as we turn ourselves about.

In June, Tim mows the circle
from the outside in.
We move close together
and it all begins again.

CAT HAIKUS

Pounce. Bite dust chipmunk
Toss in air, bat him around
Can't bring in house

        I don't know pole cats
        I only wanted to play
        Hate tomato juice

                Knock down wine glasses
                I am Sir Roger, take that
                They yell Pissant creep

I am the Boss cat
Mafiaso godfather
Tuxedo cool cat

        Guinness does not come
        They call him every evening
        Nose rub friend. Miss him

                They play their fiddles
                I glare - my ancestors yowl
                I am going out

Sleep in sun on mat
Sometimes in attic corner
Where nobody knows

        Stay outside in cold
        Some of us die all alone
        Can't make up my mind

                I am an old cat
                Want to die in master's arms
                Getting ready now

WOODBOX

It stayed empty all summer
and into autumn.
Around the fall equinox
there was a slight nip
down to 35
so I garnered some kindling,
scrounged some newspaper,
got a fire going
in the old Lang.
Fetched one stick from the shed
and that lasted the night.
Same the next night,
one stick from the shed
never made it to the box,
like if we could keep the box empty
it would ward off winter,
even bring back some warmer days.
But eventually we had a frost,
had to get three sticks
before morning.
Found it easier to
keep some in the box
and soon armloads.
The crook in my left arm
becomes shaped like the letter J
and it stays that way
until next May.

OLD ROGER

Old Roger is dead and lies in his grave, goes the old song.
They planted an apple tree over his head, the apples got ripe
and they all tumbled down, then comes the old lady a-picking
them up. Old Roger gets up and gives her a thump.

My fruit trees are forty years along now, twice
that apple time. *(Like a dog has 7 years to our one.)*
They did well even as semi-dwarfs, lots of apples for cider,
winter keeping, mix with peanut butter, dates and bananas.
Give surplus to neighbor's pig, get bacon in return.

Pour a little scrumpy around the roots in January to cheer
them up, but there's been nothing for several years now, oh
maybe an apple here and there. Pears do well every other
year or so.

But the trees look great, if a bit gray and gnarled. Blossom
each spring, keep plugging away. I stand here, arms
spread out like a tree, as in the song, waiting for old Roger
to get up, give her a thump.

MAPLE

Had an early run that year in January of all times for
god's sake, regular thaw for about a week, some
farmers southern part of the state, lucky, got in some
taps and made a few quarts. Then it locked up for a month,
had another run mid February for a few days, couple more
farmers got into the game before things froze up again and
everyone waited for March. Everything usually wraps up
end of March but not that year. Another good run right into
April filling the pails to overflowing. Then the mercury
plummeted before we could gather, had to take a stick,
plunge it through the ice into the unfrozen pale brown sugary
sap at the bottom and this would stick to the club and in turn,
freeze. End of the day had a maple lollypop. That's nothing,
up in Quebec they carry on until end of April, first of May
even up there where the maples give way to birch. Place there,
St. Pierre on Ile d'Orleans, cold sunny day middle of April,
three feet of snow on the ground, the Charlevoix Mountains
purple across the St. Lawrence. Small sap house, l'homme
inside sitting on an elevated padded chair over the evaporator,
all you see are his feet through the steam. Sits there, pipe going,
toddy in one hand, wooden spoon in other stirring the boil
below, getting down occasionally, goes outside spreads
thickened syrup into troughs of snow, or scatters it like leather
aprons on the drifts. Folks roll it up onto spoons, stand there
sucking it up, tee shirts, mindless of the cold, it is their rite of
spring, singing chansons. Then into the hotel for supper, tables
all set, fresh flowers, tall slim wine bottles filled with light
amber syrup which goes on or in everything, potatoes, eggs,
ham, bacon, salad, coffee, rum. Then they dance, maybe have
more sucre d'erable. And lots of water.

LAWN?

What lawn?
I like it unkempt,
just a path to the house
through the tall grass.
Get wet sometimes after a rain but so what.
Besides, tall plantings give the illusion
of a short house close to the ground,
so the landscapers say.

Feller at work offered me a boat,
a small boat, a peapod, needed work.
I'm not good at that,
have no pond stream nearby,
live 20 miles inland from Belfast.
Told my daughter and she said
Bring it home Dad, put it on the lawn,
everyone coast of Maine
has a boat on their lawn.
Put that lobster crate in it,
the one you keep back of your pick-up.
Better yet I could patch it up,
fill it with water.
Good place for my ducks.

LILAC A Found Poem

I wanna wake up in New Hampshire
where the purple lilacs grow
where the sun comes a-peepin'
into where I'm sleepin'
and the song bird says "hello" ... hello

I wanna wander through the wildwoods
where the fragrant breezes blow
and drift back
to New Hampshire
where the purple lilacs grow.

Dad planted a lilac under that massive bull pine, dropping needles
for mulch, all that acidity in the soil, but it never bloomed for thirty
years, never bloomed, just a stick Mom said, and I said to Rick,
my brother, I said Let's move the damn thing but he said No, Dad
wanted it there so that's where it should be, but Dad never saw it
bloom, so he died and now Mom's getting ready to check out and I
come up from Boston every week to keep her from choking on her
dinner and the osprey has flown over, the Scarlet Tanager, the eagle,
foxes, deer, all come to say goodbye and I wake up this morning I
can't believe what I'm seeing, the lilac has bloomed.

10

HOW TO MAKE HARD CIDER SCRUMPY

Go to the local whiskey wholesaler and pick up a stout sixty
gallon oak barrel, charred inside, maybe even have some of the
old stuff swishing around. Take her to the cider mill, fill her up
with the juice of the Baldwin or Golden Russet. Nothing else.

Roll it down the bulkhead and set it on its side in the cellar so
the bung is facing up. Measure the distance between bung and
ceiling rafter. Cut a 4 x 4 one inch longer, and jam it between
the bung and rafter. Tie logging chains around the barrel. Hitch
them to hooks set in the foundation, and your house will shake
all winter.

How To Make It Last

Tap the barrel in mid-March to help you through the sugaring.
Keep a bottle hidden in the wood pile for to offer sparingly
to the passersby. If it appears as though it might be getting scarce,
maybe not last through haying, don't offer any. Tell them you
drank it all. Give them rum instead.

HOW TO GRAB LEAVES

You have to understand that this is about getting leaves for mulch
in the garden. Make sure you get them from your own property,
not have to import them. Do it on a rainy day or at least when the
leaves are wet. Use a fan-shaped lawn rake to get the leaves into
piles. Don't pick them up in a wheelbarrow. You just can't get
very many in one. Use a leaf grabber. Take two poles, six feet
long, an inch square or round, an old sheet or blanket, canvas, six
feet long and four feet wide. Staple on long side to one pole and
the other side to the other pole. Approach the pile. Nudge one
side under the pile with your foot. Keep nudging. Reach over the
top with the other pole and grab the leaves, reaching around
underneath to touch the other pole and pull it all up, tucking
under your arms. Deposit the leaves where you want them in the
garden. Cover with old hay or garden refuse like squash
vines, bean vines, zinnia stalks, cosmos stalks, to weight down
the leaves, keep them from blowing away so you won't have to
be grabbing them again.

FROST HEAVES
A Northern New England Season December to April

> *"Frost heavies are hard to see at night.*
> *Just don't go out at night,*
> *not this time of year.*
> *Frost heavies are nocturnal."*

from UNTIL I FIND YOU
John Irving

What happens is water seeps under the macadam, freezes and pushes up, cracking the surface. When you see the sign FROST HEAVES it means the road ahead has bumps, or heaves but it also is telling you that frost does the heaving. Each year they seem to get worse. Some folks remember from year to year but they don't put a label on it like wine. Most roads have a crown at the yellow line so water will drain off to the ditch. This season causes ridges in the center of each lane. The oil pans and mufflers on low slung cars scrape these eruptions. It is a noisy time. Gravel roads are free of this nuisance. They do have some pot holes and washboard, but if you drive fast enough you hit the first one and bounce over the rest. Best way to deal with the old heaves on tar roads is to drive with the left side of car on the ridge of the winter crown and the right side on the shoulder. Takes twice as long to get to the village. The freeze buckles the road and you have to Buckle Up.

CLEAR AND DRY

Excuse me, did I just hear you say you are a weather forecaster?
At the local station? Well I'm going to send you a bill, don't know
yet for how much, have to do some research yet, but you'll get it
don't you worry. I am a dairy farmer, or was. Lost all my hay two
summers running because you predicted clear and dry and I believed
you. Lost it all goddamit. Couldn't afford to buy hay from Quebec,
so I had to sell the herd, go to sweeping floors at the school, jesus,
but I'm gonna bill you for it, get my cows back, clear and dry my
ass.

THIS IS THE DAY WE'VE BEEN WAITING FOR

Yes, hello? Yes, I'd like to speak with the weather guy.
Yes, thanks, (she put me on hold) humdedum dum de dum.
Yes George, this is Joseph Slenk. Did I understand you to just say
a few minutes ago on the weather that this is Indian Summer?
You didn't? Well what did you say? Indian summer weather.
Well that's better. Why do I ask? Well those assholes down in
Boston whenever they do the weather this time of year any cold
night and warmish day after Labor Day is Indian Summer. They
don't know diddley. What do I think is Indian Summer? Well it
comes after Thanksgiving or around then, leaves all down, been a
good freeze or two. Ground maybe even frozen. Could be it
snowed once or twice. Then you get a day like today, soft and hazy,
run around in tee shirts and shorts. Like those guys they don't know
shit about living in the north. Well I'm glad you agree and we're all
on the same page here.

CANNED CORN

Earl grew a few acres of sweet corn alongside of his cow corn.
The cannery came with a John Deere harvester (could hardly fit in
the field), left the broken stalks for silage.

Earl's wife took in floors to wash when she wasn't being nurse.
Earl worked at the cannery to supplement the milk checks.
His corn, as well as Fecteau's, Sweeney's, Batchelder's, Nichol's,
all mixed together in the vats. All canned together on the belt.
Sealed into the tins from the same batch. Labels glued on at the
end, IGA, FIRST NATIONAL, STOP & SHOP, SS PIERCE.

SOLSTICE SONNET

December twenty one is winter solstice.
Sometimes tee shirt weather, most times cold.
The strength of winter's weight is well upon us
as we struggle single file through wind and snow.

Making our way to the distant ancient grove
deep in the forest where the bonfire holds
for the northern conifer Ents to move
around the altar like cowled monks of old.

A cedar smudge is lit and mother nature
trembles in her boots, thinks, Foiled again.
The directions are blessed, the soul, the sky,
the earth, beavers, crows, Percherons and then
an elder lights a wand to torch the pile
and the sun begins to lighten up the sky.

SQUINTING

a knot in the
pine paneling

becomes an
exotic amber parrot

long plumage
hanging

small head
big eye watching

birds outside
the bathroom window

remembering her
one short flight

DOG DAYS

Them doggies come galumphin towards us, tails
wagging, big smiles. Them goldens, them springers.
Wouldn't it be nice if everyone would greet like that,
happy to see everyone. Like to have one or two but
being itinerant, on the road all the time, have to put
them in a kennel. Cats are cool can fend for themselves.
Won't speak to you when you come home but hey.
Doggies need to be kenneled. They cry as we drive
away. Can't do it. Won't put them through all that.
Like the way I feel when you drive off August evenings
near end of summer crickets. I'll be a good doggie, sit
when you say, smile when I see you, wag the tail.
When the legs won't work right, put me on a leash,
take me with you, but please no kennel.

DOG EARED

You marked page 47. Nothing untoward there, maybe the
phone rang or someone rapped at the door? Or page 57...you had
finished your glass of wine and it was time for supper? You canine
cornered page 70. Probably nodded off with the book on your
chest, time for bed.

I generally use book marks when I can find them. Not for this
book though. I like finding my place, reading passages over until
I catch up. I marked page 79 where Howard watches George
make a little birch bark canoe to use as a pyre for a dead mouse.
I am hoping to come to a place that needs marking for any of the
above reasons, to find it already dog eared by you. It will be
double dog eared, a golden Cocker Spaniel, head tilted just so.

SPICE

This kid is going along
the sidewalk in town.

He has the Down Syndrome,
wearing a Yankees baseball cap,
a yellow sweatshirt,
blue down vest,
jeans, white sneakers.

Got a job delivering flowers
to the bank, lawyers, like that.

Holding a bunch
in front of his face,
can just see his eyes
between bib and bloom,
his nose buried deep
into the red carnations.

SAND BETWEEN TOES

Now that Crocs and Divas have been invented, one can go
swimming anywhere no matter how rough or rocky. You still get
some sand between the toes, but that's ok. When I was a kid I
didn't mind the sand. Stay there all summer for all I cared.
Go barefoot all the time. My daughter Heidi would "…live in
her swimsuit for the rest of the day."

When I got older and the sand bothered me, I would stand at the
water's edge, one foot in the pond, the other on dry beach,
shoes and towel in hand. I would balance on the foot on land,
swish the foot in the water to rinse the sand away, then make a
figure four of myself, dry the wet foot and slip on the shoe,
do a U'y, put the shod foot on terra firma, swish the other foot
and repeat the process. I can just see me doing that now.

Nice when you can come out of the water and trot up to the porch
where there is a bucket of water for the rinsing, then pad over
to a chair to let them dry.

Best though is down there to Oak Bluffs on Martha's Vineyard.
Sandy and wet, you get up to the park and walk about a quarter
mile on the lawn, moist with morning dew, which does the job.
Get to a bench, sit in the sun to dry, clean out most of whatever
sand is left between the toes, put on the shoes. Dig out the
particles later, sort of like scratching an itch.

FOX ON THE BEACH

trotting slowly before us. You tried sneaking up on it.
He would stop to turn and look, catching you in mid-track,
looking like a winged bowsprit figure, or a limbo dancer, or
balanced on one foot, an egret ready to fly. Finally he tired of
this game, loped away down the beach, suddenly vanishing
into the roses. We found several trails going into his lair but no
sight of him. Out on the road was a young girl tossing hoops
in her yard. Told her there was a fox on the beach. "Yeah, he's
cheeky that one."

MODEL A FORD/VW

Wouldn't it be great if you could take one of those
old Model A Ford sedans, say a '30 or '31, heist the
engine out and replace it with an air cooled VW Bug
motor. That was the trouble with those Model A's.
Their radiators were so sensitive, leak at the slightest bump,
freeze up, pump would go.

So you drop in the air cooled rig, keep the old radiator, it gives
the A that charm. Keep the gas tank where it is right under
the dasher so you won't need a fuel pump. Then get someone
to hitch it up so it has the front wheel drive, and by god you'll
have a doozer of a rig. Oh yeah, be sure to paint it Hawaiian
bronze.

LEAF

October walk in the woods, teacher said,
"Now children, please write a poem about this."
They all did, even the pets...*brown - down
reds – beds, all - fall* etc.

Not Sharon, class under achiever. She put an orange
leaf in her pocket, took it home, pressed it onto yellow
paper, coated it with clear wax, etched her poem in blue...

*Oh oh
here I go
falling down
with all my friends.*

Tried to get her to read it. Nope. Don't want to.
Said she liked to look at it but not spoil it by reading
it out loud.

VISIT

I drove eight hours to visit my son. He made breakfast, bacon and eggs, raisin toast, coffee. Went across the road to browse in the used books barn. Found an early Dylan Thomas. Stopped to get a tray of Niagara grapes to eat on the way home. Then to a winery for a sip of Niagara wine before the sun was over the noon mark. Went to his place of work with handicapped children. We played a grand march for them. Nathaniel had a Down Syndrome boy on one arm, and an autistic girl on the other while pushing a wheelchair. Everyone wanted to dance with him. After, we had coffee and a snack at his favorite place in town. Graham crackers with peanut butter, chocolate spread and banana. Stepped out the door and down the steep steps into the gorge. Waterfall tumbling down into the city. I sat on a stone slab. "Oh," I said, "this is what I really came here to see. Wow." Nathaniel was standing just above me, kicking stones into the water. There was no spray, but there was moisture on his cheeks. Just kicking stones.

WOOL SUITS

When he was four he wore those knitted red and green two piece
wool suits with bright shiny buttons along the collar bone.
He outgrew them about the time he was ready for knickers.
He had two pair, one tweed that came down over the cuffs at the knee,
stockings went over the cuffs or under, didn't matter, couldn't see
them anyway. The other pair was blue corduroy that went up straight
from the cuffs, socks went either over or under. If over meant they
might slide down, if under, then the cuffs showed and he really liked
this way best, the tight feeling of the elastic cuff, the zip zip zip sound
new corduroy knickers would make as he walked to school. *Years
later he would think of that, always picture himself in the same place
about half way up the block from home although they must have made
that sound everywhere.* But either way was good in the neighborhood,
so he would have them one way one day and the other way the next
day. Then he was ready for long trousers. Wore them long except
when playing football at which time he rolled them back up to the
knees to be like the Eagles at BC. Otherwise no problem with
socks, they went under the pants legs although some kids
stuffed their pants down inside their socks but they got laughed at so
there was no problem here, no choice to have to make.

DO YOU EVER

think sometimes
if there is
someone out there
who is getting fucked
& they are
imagining
it is you
who is
doing the job
& don't you
wish they would
let you
in
on the fun

YARD SALE

When god invented sex she put a plan in place to deal with surplus semen. For in order to guarantee propagating the species there has to be a surplus. So she invented stimulants like bikinis and cleavage, egg whites to thin out the semen, thus spreading the wealth.

Then came the yard sale but before that, K-Marts and Wal-Marts to provide the fodder for future yard sales, and Detroit for annual contributions to junk yards, and storage bins for keeping future yard sales well stocked.

Surplus is good, makes jobs for everyone. Can say the employment index is healthy.

TAO – SEX BY THE SEASON

Day O, day ay o
Daylight comes and I wanna go home

Tao does it by the season. Not at all in the winter? Spring may be
its most frequent. Whoopee. "...once a week, and the elderly even
less than that." Give me a break. You've got to be kidding.
Cooped up all winter and we can't go to it more than once a week
come spring? Not to worry, I'm 85 so overindulgence will not
be an issue. We can find the proper balance and not fall out of bed.

LOOKING BACK

Don't recall looking forward to diapers
or ahead to knitted suits either.
Nor back to them once I got to knickers,
or over shoulder when I earned my trousers.

How I combed my hair seemed important,
shaving, color sox, change of voice.
I had heard of sex but it hadn't
happened to me yet, but then oh boy,

when it did I thought of nothing else.
This went on for years before changes
has me remembering sexy tussels,
eyes are bigger than the member ranges.

Now when I see diapers on a line,
I think Oh lord not this all over again.

HERE

your letters
come to me

because
you aren't

& I wonder
how long before

(if/&/or
ever)

they won't
have to

because
you are

GREAT NEW HAMPSHIRE WHIRLWIND

In 1821, a tornado cut a swath from
Croydon, NH, through
New London and Warner.
"The tornado ended in the woods of Boscawen"
dumping its debris in Canterbury
where I later built a house.

Meanwhile, I make do with myself. The trunk of me is a tornado. Some days it is white as the driven snow. Others it is green and yellow. To many it would seem black. It is made up of multiple suction vortices that whirl around inside of me, bumping into each other, growling, snarling and spitting, and creating havoc along the way. Sometimes these vortices get away to run out and play in the yard. They dangle like pendants from a chandelier, hopping and skipping about, waving their arms, dancing to Wind That Shakes The Barley. They whip around me taking ten turns to my one, narrow little things, rotating all the while churning up the ground.

I am hoping one will come across the field here. A small whispy see through kind of one with no vortices. My multiples will go out and surround her, and we will collide and wrassle and merge.

FOREPLAY

The time spent anticipating an event is 75% or is it 80 % of the
enjoyment of whatever, ski-ing, going to a movie, eating, sex.
Take ski-ing, you get the skiis down from the rafters, wax them
up, arrange them on the rack, drive to the resort thinking about the
runs, have a coffee before you ride the lift, freezing your ass off,
and then it's over in an instant as you tear down the hill. Or eating...
you think about a nice swordfish, and after you've devoured it you
wonder what the hell was that all about? But sex. You can really
get off thinking about that. You can be like little Jack Horner who
sat in a corner, amusing himself by abusing himself and jerking
off in his hat. Or you can think about tits inside and then outside
sweaters, and then you think enough is enough and you go for
it but she says no not yet, you haven't anticipated long enough,
or rousingly enough, go back to your fantasies, and you do so
happily because this is ok. Then once you do get it on, you can
stretch it out forever because you are an old duffer and have
had prostate troubles as well...radiation and all that shit, so you
have a delayed coming which is ok with her because she can look
up as long as you can pull grass.

CAN'T GET ENUFF OF THE STUFF IN THE MUFF

sang Robert Burns. That's how it is when you're a kid full of piss and vinegar, wondering where and when your next piece is coming from. Occupies much of your day and night. Then somehow love enters the mix, getting everyone in a twit. So of course it leads to marriage and a settling down. Things level off, get it regularly, don't have to worry where it's coming from. Build a house, have some kids, grow a garden, even some cultivated oats. Get some gray hair, look for a bit on the side. Survive all that, kids grow up, go away. No need for garden, it becomes overgrown with bittersweet. So once again you can't get enuff, with emphasis on *get*. It has nothing to do with availability, but rather just plain ability. So you start setting music to Little Boy Blue come blow your horn.

"THE SHOT HIT A ROCK, SPLIT IT IN TWO, KILLED BOTH FOXES"

from BERT & I stories

What a christly shot. Kid couldn't have been more'n thirteen.
Went straight through the doe's heart, out the other side through
skipper's 'n out the other side, christ knows where it would have
gone hadn't hit a rock. Went back into skipper, killed him twice.
Ought to know, was right there. Had to tag skipper myself else the
kid've lost his license. Can't kill two deer, even if it is with one shot.
Who would believe it, hard enough time myself and I was there,
forget the warden. And the thing of it is I mean the poor kid can't
even talk about it. Like I'm telling you, his uncle, but jesus god
on a crutch, gets two for one first shot ever at a deer and can't even
brag about it to his buddies, lose his license, jesus what's the use.
What if the buck had been there and he got three for one. Talk about
protecting your young. Hell that's what I did, I jumps in and tags the
skipper. I mean what a christly shot.

SKATING

One cold windy day January
20 below but sunny,
Dad and I skated
from Garvin Falls in Bow
all the way down to
Amoskeag Falls in Manchester.

We swooped in wide sweeps
over beautiful black ice,
the wind at our backs.

On the way back up river
we skated into a cove there in Hooksett
out of the wind.

We could see a golden fish
beneath the ice.

Dad took his hatchet
(he thought of everything)
chopped a hole,
Dropped a hook and line
(had that too, don't remember what he used for bait)
soon had it flopping on the ice.

I got a fire going
near the shore
and we cooked it up.

STE. JEROME vs STE. AGATHA

Neither team has done well this season in the Eastern Quebec Junior League, both sporting losing records. But here they are at it in the Ste. Agatha Arena. The boys from Ste. Jerome got off to a quick lead early in the first period and led 2-0 going into the second. Ste. Agatha tallied at the 10 minute mark, but Roland Marcoux got it back a minute later and Ste. Jerome led 3-1. Five seconds into the last period, Belanger slapped one into the Ste. Jerome net making it 3-2 and that is the way it held until the last minutes. A delayed penalty was called against Ste. Jerome, interference. Ste. Agatha pulled their goalie and, mon dieux, they scored. 3-3. Play resumed and same thing, Ste. Jerome got called again, for tripping this time, delayed, out came Marcel and Ste. Agatha put themselves ahead from a scramble in front of the net. 4-3. Ten seconds remaining and Ste. Jerome pulls their goalie only to have Soucy slip one by the defense and into the empty net at the siren. 5-3, Ste. Agatha.

M&Ms

You open a small package of M&Ms and dump them on the table, arranging them by color in separate piles...red, yellow, orange, blue, brown and green. Start with the reds. You squeeze one. If it breaks eat it. Squeeze another. If it doesn't crack open or break, set it aside. Keep this up until you have eaten all the red ones except the winner who doesn't break. Do the same with all the colors. Then you have a round robin between the winners, all of them play the others until you have a final winner. Then you eat it.

IN THE 50s

After the game (5-1 Canadiens), both teams boarded the
11:15 from North Station in Boston, headed for Montreal,
passing through Concord, New Hampshire at 1:00 am.

Time for a coffee and pie at the all-night diner while waiting for
arrival.

The train pulled in. Clanking empty milk cans from Hoods
tossed off to be stacked for farmers to pick up.

Through steamy windows I could see Les Canadiens, Richard,
Geoffrion, Plante, and Bruins, Pearson, Mackell, Toppazzini,
playing cards, reading newspapers, napping.

The whistle blew, the train pulled out, headed north into the
March night.

IPH

Whenever I get up to bat I always try to get an inside the ballpark homerun (IPH). Triples are good but I'd rather go for the IPH. I have four of them lifetime, all hit in Fenway Park. I played for the St. Louis Browns when I whacked the first one, hitting the edge of the wall in center field where the bleachers join the leftfield green monster. It bounced way back onto the field and I came home standing up.

The next one (I was on the Red Sox then) was a sneaky hit pulled into the leftfield corner sticking in the drainpipe there. It was a close call me having to nose dive under the catcher.

The third IPH came playing for the Washington Senators. A liner inches over first base landed fair, curved foul, caromed off the right field fence, rolled all the way to the bullpen. There was a drizzle, the ball and field were slippery. Even so I still had to slide for it.

The last one was a doozer. I was back with the Browns again. It was an inside the infield homer (IIH). We had a man on second. I hit the first pitch, a low scorcher down the first base line, striking the first baseman on the ankle, bouncing off into the Bosox dugout, indeed rolling all the way down the passageway into the shower room. Of course the first baseman was writhing on the ground so the pitcher had to go after it. By the time he found it, the man on second had scored and I had rounded third headed home. He, the pitcher, tripped on the steps coming out so the throw was just wide enough to allow me to score.

Like I say, I like triples too. Actually my IPHs are all triples stretched into homers. My triples (758 lifetime) are all stretched doubles, one of them a ground ruler that went under the garage door in center field. I don't do singles.

AT THE KICKING DONKEY IN BROKERSWOOD, WILTSHIRE

I'm having a pint of the local bitter, and this guy beside me says
Hey I see by your bells that you are a morris dancer. Well you
probably won't believe this, but I have a buddy, he's sort of a scholar,
and he says that morris dance was invented by Maurice Richard, the
stick wielding hockey player for the Montreal Canadiens back in the
fifties. Rene Lecavalier announcing the games at the forum would say
"There goes Maurice dancing through the line." I can see you don't
believe me. I have a hard time with it myself, but that's what he says.

WHY THE EYNSHAM MORRIS SIDE

dances Brighton Camp to the chune Girl I Left Between Me so
fast is because of the feathers they wear in their green felt hats that
point straight back, not up, but back, giving the impression of speed.
It helps that the mouth harp, key of C, double reed, is going at 116
metronome, even though the dancers are wearing mud caked boots,
but mostly it's the feathers.

UNITE

The good folk of Padstow in Cornwall
would if they could do the hobby horse
on May 1 each year unless it falls
on a Sunday, then Monday of course.

We do it here northeast stateside May first,
except Sunday. Get the old accordion
out, the drums, beer to quench the thirst.
Dress the kids in white, forsythia garlands.

Unite for summer is a-coming in
even though there still is snow around.
We are singing it at ten AM
and they at four PM across the pond.

What grips us, is we are doing it
same time they are for a few minutes.

PHOTO OF SHAKER SISTERS
AT THE SEASIDE 1923

Four of them
standing in a close knit circle,
their bonnets
gleaming in the sun.

their long skirts

their high black shoes

One is tall,
has a sharp nose,
long dark hair
gathered in a net,
blowing in the sea wind.

They are humming,
I am sure they are humming.

If they put their arms
around each other's shoulders
they would be dancing
a Basket Quadrille.

They must be humming
Lovely In The Dances.

MY JOB

is such that I show kids how to do old-time New Hampshire barn dances like the Virginia Reel. I get them up into lines facing their partners and have them circle left, then right, all in and out, swing their partners, get into lines again and start the corners bowing. The trick is, I call and play harmonica same time, talking out of the corner of my mouth, stop playing, chant the call, same key (G), then keep on playing, picking up where I left off, sometimes adds extra beats, but I use crooked French chunes so it doesn't matter. I have what I call my "mate," a kid or the teacher banging a tambourine. My harmonica is a double reed key of G, loud. Sometimes I use a holder for my harp like Bob Dylan, but sans cigarette. This allows me to hold and beat a tambourine at the same time. I get overtime for this act.

So that's it, it's what I do. Lucky to get work in schools these days, has to be curriculum oriented. I suppose you could say what I do is school geared, math, forward four steps and four back, social skills, history, music. To me dancing is a way of courting, which is a life skill. Everyone likes to swing. Even third grade boys.

McQUILLEN "and the music and that's how it is now"

This accordion player is a laughing fellow
with steel gray hair, bribing the bellows.

He coaxes and listens to the Irish in it,
falls of water, hills of granite,

weather brown barns, evergreen tree.
He roars with laughter & slaps his knee,

His music blends with the fiddle man,
the caller, the piano, the summer dancers

with taps on their shoes, fresh from the farms,
the woolen mills.

                    He tattooed his arms.

Looks like he's taking a nap on his box,
but what he is doing is coaxing talk,

getting it going like a spinning top,
you can hear it out in the parking lot.

MAY DAY

1.

The village pub (*The Maypole*) closed and changed
into a private house some years ago.
The pole used to be taller but the deranged
sod who bought the pub, objected so
if the pole fell over, crush his house.
Good lord, If you're worried a maypole
is going to fall on your house, why choose
it, get a country place out by Heathrow.

But it hasn't stopped the celebrations.
The Wiltshire County Council even tried
to declare the pole a traffic infraction,
but it's still there in middle of the road.

And we will dance around it on May Day,
drink our pints and dance the Shepherd's Hey.

2.

There was a morris dancer, Denis McGee
every May Day danced the Queen's Delight
in the courtyard of Oxford University
at one minute past the hour of midnight.

He did the capers, the back steps with full grace.
The fiddle screeched when he did the splits,
all the while a big grin on his face,
giving all the ladies there the fits.

The University Rag Week caught all this
on their cover, somehow adding a broomstick
strategically placed between his
wide spread legs with bold print caption fixed.

Hip hip hooray, hooray, the First of May,
Good old outdoor sex begins today.

3.

Then old Denis thought of a May Day tour which
would take in all the pubs on Salisbury Plain,
similar to Kemp's trot from London to Norwich,
a pint in each made from the local grain.

They hoisted one at the King's Head and then
the Haunch of Venison in Salisbury.
Another on the outskirts of Stonehenge,
by now they were in the throes of merry.

Indeed one of them had got quite pissed.
He danced with a heavy leftward lurch.
Stumbled through Bleddington's Hey Diddle Dis
and capered off the street into a church.

On a table, the open book for guests.
He signed "Hip hip hooray" you know the rest.

I AM RAFTERY

(Transcription of a translation (Hyde) of a Gaelic poem by Anthony Raftery)

I am Raftery the fiddler,
The wandering bard.
My eyes have no sight
But light is my heart.

Going west on my journey
By the light of my soul,
So tired and weary
To the end of my road.

I've long spindly legs
And a shock of red hair,
A way with the women
And with whiskey I fear.

I wander the roads
Through Galway I go,
All searching for love
On my way to Mayo.

Behold me now
With my back to a wall;
Playing music
For an empty hall.

HOW TO DO A GRAND CHAIN

I rousted myself up,
got dressed for a Saturday,
black trousers, plaid shirt, red tie,
tweed jacket, visored cap,
all set to go to the local
to tie on a small one,
then to the Finn Hall,
upstairs one step at a time,
a wedding in full swing.
They were doing a Paul Jones
and I got swept into a grand chain
without a partner,
pulled by the right,
yanked by the left,
hand over hand like swimming,
more like dog paddling,
Came around to the door
and detoured out
down the stairs
careful not to fall in a heap,
outside to the streets of Ludlow.
O boy, now that I can
do a grand chain,
means I can go to that
dance in Gassetts.
Isn't that a great name,
I love it, roll it on the tongue,
fix the gasket on my car,
fetch my girl lives in Tisket,
that little village there in Tasket.

HOW CONTRA DANCING WAS INVENTED

Started off as a cash crop. Had to entertain them summer folk on
Saturday nights. Got Uncle Walter to show us the figures 'n steps
to them old contrys and quadrilles. We called 'em square dances.
Hollis & Quint played their flute & fiddle. They'd get Arno on
his guitar, and go down to that abandoned cider mill, had that
brook running underneath it, smell of pomace and rotting wood.
Sit there in the lantern light, pass a bottle around, play them
old dance tunes with that great echo.

Uncle Walter's nephew would sit in a dark corner. Couldn't see
him, quiet feller. Surprised everyone by lilting out in his flute-
fiddle voice, chanting the changes to Hull's Victory like he'd been
doing it all his life. He was a natural. They pressed him into
service at the very next dance.

You know how the story goes from here. How the hippies came
to the dances with their patchouli oil and bare feet, how they
didn't like the word "square," and how they discovered some
were contras. We heard one of them tell someone, "It's not square
dancing, it's contra dancing. It's not square dancing, it's contra
dancing."

The rest is history except that there are still some of us old folks
up here who like to say we're going to the square dance.

FIDDLE CAMPS

Fiddlers Mellie Dunham and George Overlock,
Mainers of the first hair, had about thirty tunes in their
repertoire: Turkey in the Straw, Irish Washerwoman,
Soldier's Joy, Campbells Are Coming and like that,
for the contras Lady of the Lake, Boston Fancy, Mountain
Ranger, Haymakers. They swapped those tunes around for
those dances, to do the job. Then someone, lord knows who,
came across Cincinnati Hornpipe and Top Of Cork Road Jig,
and dances that went with them. More music was discovered,
more dances, more people to play them. New tunes and dances
written like McQuillen's Squeezebox, Nantucket Sleighride,
which made for an enormous surplus of music and dances
which then necessitated the advent of the use of medleys,
(three chunes, or more, per contra,) but even so there was not
enough days in the week for them to play all the music for
all the dances, so the need for fiddle camps arose, followed
by dance camps and organic farms to feed them all, and now
everyone is a fiddler, dancer, farmer or all of the above at once
and nobody has time to do anything else like go to war or shit
like that.

DOWNTOWN

The kid couldn't have been
twelve, if that,
was playing his fiddle
on the street
in downtown Portsmouth
across from the brewery there,
had an open fiddle case
making good money
from the passersby.
He was playing hornpipes
in a medley of three,
had started with Quindaro on G,
switched to Forester's on D,
finished with Lamplighters on A.
Two cops sauntered by to listen.
"Do you have a license?" one asked.
"No, I'm too young to drive" the boy replied.

"I mean, do you have a permit to play here?"

"No."

"Well, it's against the law to
solicit here without a license,
we'll have to take you downtown."

The boy said, "I am downtown."

DANCE TO YOUR DADDY

Dance to yer daddy
My little laddie
Dance to yer daddy
My little man

Old Scottish Song

For Corinne

Dad used to play fiddle for us in the kitchen. I chorded on my
toy piano. Mom peeling potatoes Dad had brought in from the
garden. We danced around, Junior twirling and slapping his
bass. It slipped once, landed on Dad's bald spot, blood dripped
down his face. Never missed a note, cussed a bit, but never
missed a note.

Junior twirled his life away.

Loretta was the dancer, followed Dad wherever he played.
Old Wristy everyone called him. I followed Mom's footsteps,
became a musician's widow, marrying a trumpeter. My fingers
did my dancing through the pages of my stories. Dad's gone now.
Junior's playing bass for him over there. Mom's gone too, still
doing potatoes, same apron I'll bet. Tetta's knees gave out. She
sits by the window, drumming her fingers on the table, some tune
of Dad's. My man's gone now, probably teaching Gabriel the
Devil's Dream. I try to recall church hymns but Dad's music is
all that I hear.

CODE TALKERS DANCING

for Pfc. Bob McQuillen, USMC

A dozen or so Navajo marines,
Student code talkers,
   nursing their beers after last call
   at the base canteen.
The moon shone onto the porch.
One of the Indians started lightly
Drumming out a beat,
Flat of his hand on the table top.
Thump, thump thump thump,
   thump, thump thump thump.
Slowly the others arose,
Slipped out of their jeans
   down to breechclouts,
Got into a circle
Without so much as a command
Started their ceremonial moon dance.
Shuffle, shuffle shuffle thump,
   shuffle, shuffle shuffle thump,
   to the speech of the drum
   the moon language.
Those men understood that talk.

BLUE AT THE 40TH
MARLBORO MORRIS ALE

We were kids 40 years ago,
known then as the
Canterbury Morris Minors,
a yellow Phoenix
rising from ashes
out of our blue vests.
We have kids of our own now
and we all dance together
in our deep blue
uniform we wear on the road.
Our home uniform
is more a faded Shaker blue,
a barn door blue,
a haywagon blue,
what you see around the old
New Hampshire countryside.
Some of us are fading,
not away mind you,
just a few wrinkles,
some white hair.
That's ok,
we can drink Shaker switchel.
But most important,
the blue stays with us.

The Giraffe, the Goat, the Elephant, the Lion and the Peacock are all do-
ing the Morris Dance on the Green. In the background is the Town Hall,
as you can see. All the animals have bells on their feet. They are all
dressed in costumes. They each have their own sticks and they all have
hats on. All the animals have their white pants suits on.

- SHW

AS YOU CAN SEE

Stuart was watching the Pinewoods Morris dancing on the streets of Han-
cock. You could tell he was imagining them as giraffes and horses, good
subjects for a painting. He was asked if he could do that and he said yes
but first he had other things to tend to like being the ever animal rightist,
growling at women wearing mink. Yes he would get to it but he had to
think on it while floating on Harrisville Pond, only letting you know
where he was by the water spouting from his mouth. He said he had to go
west to be a C&W singer, but before he left, he put his goat into the paint-
ing, as you can see.

Stuart Williams, Peterboro, NH,
December 2, 1950 - May 15, 2012

Wind In The Timothy

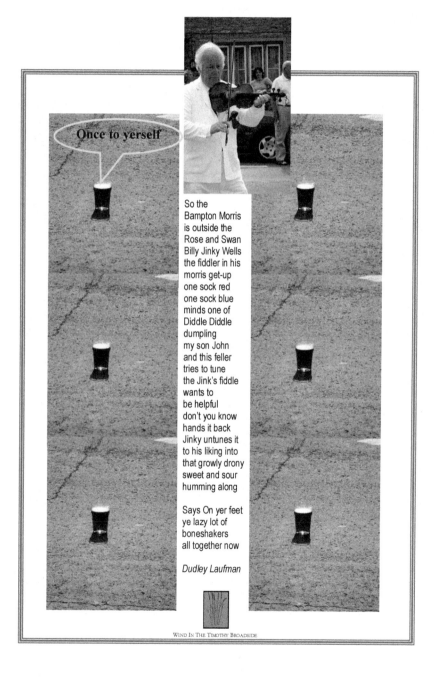

Once to yerself

So the
Bampton Morris
is outside the
Rose and Swan
Billy Jinky Wells
the fiddler in his
morris get-up
one sock red
one sock blue
minds one of
Diddle Diddle
dumpling
my son John
and this feller
tries to tune
the Jink's fiddle
wants to
be helpful
don't you know
hands it back
Jinky untunes it
to his liking into
that growly drony
sweet and sour
humming along

Says On yer feet
ye lazy lot of
boneshakers
all together now

Dudley Laufman

COME ALONG YOU LUCKY LADS, COME ALONG
Bampton in the Bush, Oxfordshire, England, Whit Monday 2004

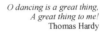

O dancing is a great thing,
A great thing to me!
Thomas Hardy

You wonder how it must be
for old athletes like Johnny Pesky,
Joe Cronin, Ted Williams,
Maurice Richard, Woody Dumart,
to have to retire their bats,
hang up their skates.
Must be the same for musicians,
or old morris dancers,
but these guys they
still go to the games, concerts,
or street shows,
most of them anyway,
for some it must be tough.
In Bampton, England for instance,
there's old Francis Shergold,
brown, wrinkled,
in full Bampton Morris kit,
pint of bitter in hand,
watches his side dance The Webbly
outside the Horse Shoe Inn.
His younger brother, Roy,
like a walnut,
best dancing fool
Bampton ever had,
passes by on the
other side of street
hoe on shoulder,
on his way to
dig in someone's orchard,
barely waves.

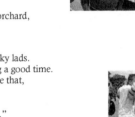

Francis saying,
"Look at them lucky lads.
Aren't they having a good time.
I used to dance like that,
wish I could now,
can't get the
old knees up can I."

Francis thinking,
I'll have another pint
then go home,
sit in the garden.

— Dudley Laufman

Wind In The Timothy Press

CLEMENT WEEKS

1750-1830

He wanted to be a dancing master. The kind that wore a green velvet jacket, travelling the countryside on foot or horseback, being fond of women and rum, sleeping under hedges, and with a pocket fiddle would teach the savages to dance the cotillion. That kind.

But that's not the way it went. He became a dancer instead. He attended Harvard to improve his stature in life. But all he really wanted to do was dance. He sold his fiddle so he could afford dancing lessons. He wrote all the contra dances down in a day book. Dances such as Black Joke, Greensleeves, Hunt The Squirrel, Hessian Dance, Lady's Breast Knot, The Lily, Nancy Dawson, Over The Hills And Far Away, Rural Felicity, Sukey Bids Me, Barrel of Sugar.

He came home from college to be a school master and help at the farm, mucking out the stables, sweating in the hayfields. He may have courted someone but never drank with rummy women or slept beneath honeysuckle dripping pollen. Fiddles floated before his eyes and he dream-danced his life away, dying the day before his sister. They were buried on the edge of Great Bay where the ebb tide does the contredances and the flowing does cotillions.

SUNDAY

Nobody can do eggs over easy like me and listen to and
hum/whistle along with Albinoni Concertos at the same time
in the wood heated room that smells like Quebec let alone walk
the bush trails like a guide or come into your place when a musics
is playing on the machine and I twirl you around to the three
quarter song nobody does that like I do and you in return turn
like no other with hair over your left eye nobody ever

D   *for LH*

A is for axe as you very well know
B is for the boys that use it so
C is for the chain saw that soon will begin
D is for Dudley with ruff on his chin

Lumberman's Alphabet

Rings on her fingers and bells on her toes,
She has music wherever she goes

Old Rhyme

She carries her fiddle into the woods and sits by a maple tree,
wood to wood, playing Bobby Shafto on the key of D. Then she
moves to a brook to play her harmonica, same tune, on her Key of G
mouth harp but in the key of D because she knows how to do that
cross keyed trick. Then on up a hill to the open top where she plays
the Bobby again on her single row melojun key of G but she plays it
on D because she likes it that way even without the one sharp.
But what gets me is I want to hear them bells on her toes.
I really do. Them bells.

MAYPOLE

A man builded a maypole,
Built it straight and strong.
The children danced around it
To the Bobby Shafto song.

Every May Day morning
Sang the Hal An Tow,
Sang Unite O let us,
And the Jolly Rumbalow.

The man fell by the wayside
He could no longer stand.
The maypole ribbons waited
For the children's hands.

His wife stood up beside him,
Stood up proud and tall,
Gathered the ribbons around the pole,
Hugged them one and all.

OLD MAN IN NURSING HOME
for Arthur Hanson

He said he played the fiddle.
I took him under my wing.
He could play Little Judy
and Haste to the Big Wedding.

I took him up to his old farm.
He brought some apples home,
stuffed into his pockets,
Baldwins and Red Romes.

Said he played for dances
in Parsonsfield of Maine.
Rode in horse and buggy
over and back again.

Said "I won't be around
when the leaves come down next fall,
so bury me in my old ground
and thank you one and all."

Snow was drifting gently
onto his graveyard patch.
He left me his old fiddle
and his golden watch.

SONG OF THE OLD DANCING MASTER

There is a fiddler lives under the hill,
He plays for the dances, jigs and reels,
   Under the maple trees.

His hair is gray, he is tall and thin,
Nary a tooth in cheek or chin,
   With nob nob nobbily knees.

His house is built of craggy stone,
Filled with friends, sometimes alone,
   And he lives on bread and cheese.

He keeps his silver in a stocking of red,
Tucked up under an old feather bed
   Where nobody ever sees.

He travels by foot or back of a horse,
His music is rough and his clothing coarse,
   His life is the sweets of the bees.

He carries his fiddle across his back
Under his cloak in an old knapsack
   Safe from the wet and freeze.

He plays his fiddle for young and old,
For the abled and not so abled I'm told,
   And he plays and dances with ease.

Children romp and skip up and down.
He scoops out a hole in the dancing ground
   And it fills up with silver you see.

He likes to play in an old farmhouse
Where the floor is sprung and lamplight glows
   And they dance the Portland Fancy.

John Paul Jones and Virginia Reel,
Morning Star and a plain quadrille
    And the lovely Sherbooke Brandy.

Paddy Whack and Off She Goes,
Opera Reel and Speed the Plow
    And other tunes like these.

His fiddle tuned with a high bass so,
And his feet beat out the staccato
    Tight as pod full of peas.

He plays for gypsies in an ivied wood.
Sits on a stump on the edge of the glade,
    Plays an old reel in G.

A gypsy in red bangs a big tambourine,
And children are dancing in a ring
    To another fiddler's key.

Stay say the youngsters, teach us new jigs.
Tarry says their fiddler tightening her strings
    And they fiddle wild and free.

He sits by the fire in the winter time
And counts his blessings three, six, nine,
    Thankful for wild gypsies.

If I were the fiddler and you were my friend,
    Come and go as you please
I'd play my fiddle at the day's end
        For you. How good that would be
        My love,
    O how good that would be.

DANCING IN COUNTY CLARE

It is Sunday night. The pub is
shaped like a horseshoe
magnet. A fiddle and
concertina play at
one end, their
music rough
like the broken
end of a
whetstone.

A dance is
in progress
where the
current moves
both ways.
The girls are
mini-skirted,
white as gulls.

The men are in
church clothes, dark
as ravens. They rise,
glide and dip, slanting in,
slapping their feet on the
cement like surf under the
cliffs at Dereen.

— *Dudley Lauman*   *Wind In The Timothy Press*

THE CROIS

Gardens were built on open rock slabs with a mix of sand, manure and seaweed and protected by stone walls six feet high to keep them from blowing away. Like putting a garden on a cement sidewalk. Wind blows so hard here, hens lay the same egg twice. I pulled a weed and asked Mr. Mullen, was it ragweed and he said with a wink, "Yer after pulling up one of me sugar beets, dear God save us."

Mrs. Mullen was weaving an orange, yellow and green crois from the back of a chair. She said "You don't have to empty the chamber pot you know, we can take care of that for you. You say you have one at home? Go away I don't believe ye. Yer a Yank, ye have two cars in yer blacktop driveway and three bathrooms I'm sure of it, outhouse my petticoat. And please leave the windows open dear for the fresh sea breezes don't ye know. And you said you wanted to see a peat fire? Well I've built one for ye, hope yer satisfied."

End of the week there was no invoice. Just the new crois wrapped in butcher's paper with a note saying, *Keep yer pants up with this and think of us. Thanks for dumping yer own chamber pot and harvesting our sugar beets. God bless.*

THE CHORUS

Sunday evening traffic jam. A farmer bringing in his cows to milk
in the middle of Ennis city. Found John Reid's house and was
greeted by a little black girl saying "Is it himself you'd be
wanting?" as John appeared behind her, a big man, blond,
more Scandi looking than Irish, saying, "This is my adopted
daughter, Sara."

After tea in the front parlor, under pictures of Kennedy and Christ,
we entered his study. There was an unruly collection of uilleann
pipes, fiddles, melodeons, tin whistles, sheet music, field event
results, (no hurling or football). Some LPs, one of them the
Tulla Céilí Band. "I have that," I said. "It's my favorite. It's where
I got Cooley's Reel." John said, "That's my band. That's me at
piano. Say now, you Yanks have a chune Chorus Jig. We have
it here only we call it The Chorus. It's a reel, you know that.
But we do have a Chorus Jig that is truly a jig. I can't bring it
to mind just this moment."

Later saying goodnight under the lamp in the mist, he took my
hand, swung it back and forth in the old Irish custom, diddling a
tune at the same time. "Deedle dum dee dum deedle dum dee dum,
that's it, the Chorus Jig, that's the one."

BREAKFAST IN ABBEYDORNEY

Just below Shannon, horse drawn carts going by the window,
cone shaped milk cans rattling.

"Dairy's just up the street," says the landlord.

"Milk goes to the chocolate industry," says the dairyman.

"Where are the cows?" I ask.

"Some just down this lane here, careful of the mud."

Farmer in knee boots hosing down the parlor,
cigarette corner of his mouth.

"From across the pond are ye now? Near Boston is it?"

Hiss of ciggie in the drain.

"Ah dear who do ye suppose will win the Stanley Cup
next week, not the Bruins the way they're playing dear god."

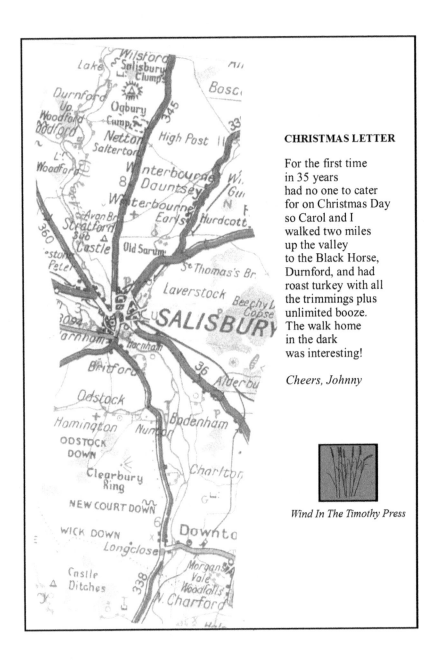

CHRISTMAS LETTER

For the first time
in 35 years
had no one to cater
for on Christmas Day
so Carol and I
walked two miles
up the valley
to the Black Horse,
Durnford, and had
roast turkey with all
the trimmings plus
unlimited booze.
The walk home
in the dark
was interesting!

Cheers, Johnny

Wind In The Timothy Press

72

BOB DUNN

He was supposed to be picking apples. I found him
part way up a tree, a Cortland, smoking
a cigarette, sort of lazily stroking
but not picking apples all around him.

"Doing any writing on this stand?"
I ask. He replies "Not yet, not yet,"
taking a drag upon his cigarette.
"Novel. Prose poem gotten out of hand.
It's about one Sean Dunn who leaves Dunlow
without saying a goodbye to his mam.
Goes to Boston and a neighbor follows
with a message to write your folks at home.
Finds him in a shit house in old Southie.
Knocks on the door saying 'Are you done?'
'Yeh.' 'Well love of Christ, write your mother.' "

ALUMNI

Big gathering, lots of white hair, spare tires.
Chancellor says, "All of those who served for
armed forces please rise to be recognized."

As a conscientious objector
I suppose I could have got up. I cleaned
up after old men who shit their britches,
broke up fights. But that wasn't what he meant.
There were others, probably farm hitches,
maybe 4-F, whatever, but only
a handful of us among the sea of vets.
Like the old North Church surrounded by
patriotic Boston, the Government
Center. No flags or bennies for us few,
but we should stand up and be counted too.

DRAFT BOARD

was in Arlington, Mass. I was working on a farm deep in the
hills of Vermont, an essential occupation. But the Arlington boys
wanted to talk to me about my CO application so I took a
Vermont Transit bus from Woodstock to Cambridge and a
street car out Mass Ave. to the draft board in Arlington. Three
cigar smoking guys fiddled with paper clips. Made me repeat my
name. "How's the weather in Vermont? You're a Quaker?" said
one. "Well that's good, there should be more of you. What do you
think of the Sox? Great homer this afternoon that George Case
stretched from a triple."

Guess they just wanted to see if I would swing a bat at anyone for
the good ole US and A. I come to find out later that my fly was
open the whole time.

CO

Call me yeller if you want
call me chicken
makes you feel better
I still ain't goin

No religious shit
Quaker or political
I'm just plain scairt
That's all

Come home with my balls shot off
prolly by one of our own men
forget it
what good is life then

BOMBING RUN

We lived on a small island off the northwest coast of Germany.
Every night the bombers would fly over, coming from
England on their way to the hinterland like thousands of fireflies
in the night sky. In the early morning they would return, flying
low over the coastal hills dropping their remaining bombs off
our shores and into our marshes, probably to lighten their loads,
maybe to avoid retribution from their superiors for not dropping
them all on Berlin. Sometimes they would wave to us. One time
a bomb must have got stuck in the bay or whatever, and when it let
go, it landed direct on a farmhouse. I am sure they didn't mean it.
They were just lads anyway.

ASHES

They arrived in a box
with a number on it.

We keep them among
the house plants,

peering out at us
through the philodendrons.

AS GHOSTS

we continue to stumble through afterlife,
trip on furniture being shown through our new
digs. When you drop things it's us warning you
about something. Our hair keeps growing,
toenails, voice on the answering machine...

THE DISPATCHER

Despeechier
To set free
Old French

He did not think of himself as a butcher, that is, one who prepares
meat for market. What he did was to arrive at the farm early
in the morning before anyone was up. Scope out the place.
Find hooks for hanging block and tackle, ropes and pulleys,
clean place on the floor, fresh sawdust. Find the animal in question,
let's say it's a bullock, get a halter on him, lead him to a pen away
from the other animals, outdoors maybe if it is summer. Brush him
down all over. Call him by his name. Scratch him behind the ears.
Put an arm around his neck. Hug him. Have the .22 close at hand.
Make eye contact. Look him in the eye. Make sure he is looking
back. Then shoot him.

NICE

That's what you would say Alan,
even to your cats.
Nice. You get everything. I don't get anything.

But you got to die first.
You got to go there before us.

You were so polite...
you even stopped and let us go ahead.
We waited for you,
but when we looked behind,
you were not there.

You went a different way.
Overhead.
It was too white to see.

JOURNEY

Morning. You up for all day? that's what my grampa used to say I
trust you slept good did your fire keep overnight mine did only
had to stir a log over onto the coals yes I would love a cup of coffee
black thank you what do you have on for today besides that shirt
headed for town later are you did I say yes to coffee looking over
your shoulder I'm staying here it's a good day outside I've things to
do I am sure you have too sorry I can't stay long

TURTLE

Recovery from surgery
was taking forever
and I complained to the doctor.
He said, Listen Dudley, You're 86,
you do a mile every day
tend your garden
play your fiddle.
Slow down a little,
lower your expectations,
you are doing fine,
better than most people your age.
Remember, the tortoise
always wins the race.
So when I got home
I'm sitting under my apple tree,
hear a rustling in the grass,
look down and there by god
was a baby snapper,
my totem
come to remind me.

BOOK BOAT

Knowing when to harvest a pear is like
knowing when to pull in the oars
gliding to a pier

from *AN ORCHARD & A GARDEN*
(Laufman)

If I buy this book now
when will I read it?

My propensity is to read books
only by the season they are set in
and by the place as well,
during *that* season and in *that* place
and a year apart to boot.

I already have two books by this guy
and they are set in New England
winter, at least after a snowfall.
So is this one, November, close
enough. Three years at least before
I get to it.

Trick is to get them all read
while I am still in the boat.
Time it so I finish the last one
as I glide in to that pier.

About the Author

As a young boy, Dudley's home was in Arlington, Massachusetts. Yet it was the people and places of New Hampshire that would reveal to Dudley the country dancing and music that would become his life's work. Working at Mistwold Farm, in Fremont, and time spent in the Monadnock Region encouraged his development as a musician and dance caller. He started calling dances at age 18 while attending Norfolk County Agricultural High School in Walpole, Massachusetts and has never looked back.

While enrolled at the Stockbridge School of Agriculture in Amherst, Massachusetts, Dudley intended to become a dairy farmer. It was here that he developed an interest in poetry and discovered the works of Hemingway, Hardy, Thomas, Burns and Sara Teasdale. Dudley began with lyrical and prose poems and his first book of poetry, "I Hear Ringing Reels" was published in 1962. Never one to write poetry as an assignment, when a poem is ready, he sets it to paper.

At age 86, Dudley is still fully engaged in a 65-year career as a dance caller for local country dances throughout New England. He plays his melodeon, harmonica and sometimes, when his fingers allow, his fiddle, at old town halls, farmer's markets, folk festivals, weddings, barn dances, kitchen junkets and for the Canterbury Morris dance team. On occasion, he is hired by elementary schools to teach old-time dances for children, a personal favorite for Dudley.

In 2009, Dudley received our country's highest honor in the folk arts for preserving traditional New England dance and music. He received an award as a National Heritage Fellow from the National Endowment for the Arts in Washington, DC. Along with an impressive list of published poetry books, Dudley has also recorded several LPs and CDs of traditional New England dance music with the group of musicians he formed in the 1970s called the "Canterbury Country Dance Orchestra." There have been two documentaries produced about Dudley's life and work: "The Other Way Back" (David Millstone, 2009) and "Welcome Here Again" (Accompany, 2017). A play written about Dudley (by Larry Siegel of Westmoreland, New Hampshire) will be premiered in September 2017 in the Monadnock Region of New Hampshire titled "The Dancing Master of Canterbury."

At the end of the day, Dudley enjoys the simplicity of a set in his garden with his cat, Merrill, on his lap, a pint of Smuttynose IPA to hand, and a good pipe on special occasions.

www.dudleylaufman.com
dudleylaufman@gmail.com

CPSIA information can be obtained
at www.ICGtesting.com
Printed in the USA
FSOW04n1834240717

9 781944 393472